Tapestries
of
Time

By the same author

With a Poem in my Pocket
Fifty Golden Years
The Patience Strong Omnibus

Tapestries
of
Time

PATIENCE STRONG

MULLER
London   Sydney   Auckland   Johannesburg

The right of Patience Strong to be
identified as Author of this work has been asserted
by Patience Strong in accordance with the
Copyright, Designs and Patents Act, 1988

This edition first published in 1991 by Muller

Random Century Group Ltd
20 Vauxhall Bridge Road, London SW1V 2SA

Random Century Australia (pty) Ltd
20 Alfred Street, Milsons Point, Sydney, NSW 2061, Australia

Random Century New Zealand Ltd
PO Box 40–086, Glenfield, Auckland 10, New Zealand

Random Century South Africa (pty) Ltd
PO Box 337, Bergvlei, 2012, South Africa

British Library Cataloguing in Publication Data

Strong, Patience
  Tapestries of time.
  I. Title
  821.912

  ISBN 0-09-174765-1

Set in Bembo by 🖊 Tek Art Ltd,
Addiscombe, Croydon, Surrey
Printed and bound in Great Britain by
Biddles Ltd, Guildford and King's Lynn

Contents

a=1st poem on page
b=2nd poem on page

Stepping Stones	7	Potpourri	28
Morning Prayer	8a	Old Age	29
Homeward Bound . . .	8b	Happy Trio	30
Home	9	Happy Home	31a
Tea-Time	10	Home Sweet Home	31b
Grandfather Clock	11	Pie-Crust	32
Gifts	12a	Christening	33
Listen!	12b	Cottage Garden	34a
Shopping	13	Decisions	34b
Fireside	14	Homecoming	35
Broken Romance	15	Long-Distance Call	36
Letters	16	Lovers' Lane	37
From a Window	17	Picnic	38
Cradles	18	Reliability	39
Slippers	19	Birthday Flowers	40
Bedside Books	20	Time	41a
Goodnight, Children	21	The Happy Day	41b
Welcome	22	Life's the Thing	42
The Spare Room	23	Bereavement	43
Roofs	24	Content	44
Sleep	25	When Troubles Come	45a
Alarm-Clock	26	Something That Belonged to Mother	45b
Jealousy	27		

This Lovely Memory	46
Just Kindness	47
Give Me the Simple Things of Life	48
Time Alone	49
The Blessing	50
Always Young	51
Mother of the Bride	52
Happy Morning	53
Make a Rainbow	54
Our Dancing Years	55
Too Late Now	56
Gardens Bring Back Memories	57
Time Will Bring It Back	58
A Window Looking West	59
Lose Yourself	60
Not Easy	61a
A Friend	61b
I Walked in Memory Lane Today	62
Take What Comes	63
One by One	64a
So Little	64b
Cosiness	65
The Instrument	66
Happiness Waiting for You	67
Give Your Love	68
The Best in Life	69
If the Heart Is Singing	70
As Roses Have Thorns	71
Happy House	72
The Haven of the Heart	73
Somebody's Tomorrow	74
Together Again	75
A Promise	76
Heart or Head	77
Let Love Speak	78
Ideal Home	79
Boy & Girl Affair	80
Condolence	81
Pictures in the Fireside	82
When I Remember You	83
Sharing	84
Fireside Rendezvous	85a
Think	85b
Try a Little Humour	86
Open the Window	87
A Wish For a Friend	88a
Time	88b
Someday Soon	89
Sweet Is the Dream	90
Thoughts Go Home	91a
Music	91b
When You Hope	92
Between the Lines	93
The Turning Point	94
The Tapestry of Time	95

Stepping Stones

Birthdays are like stepping stones –
    where Time's wide stream goes rushing by.
Sometimes in the sunlit shadows,
    sometimes in the deeps they lie . . .
But whether set in whirling pools
    or islanded in quietude,
we must stand and face the future
    in a high and happy mood.
Knowing God will take us forward
    if we trust Him without fear . . .
Every step a new adventure;
    every stone another year.

Morning Prayer

God bless my little home this day, before I start anew,
and guide my hands and give me strength for all I have to do.
May there be smiles and happy thoughts without a single tear
and no cross word creep in to mar the pleasant atmosphere.

And should some trifling thing go wrong to drag my spirits down,
lift me above all petty strife and smooth away my frown.
And when the day is ended, I'll be waiting in my place
to welcome home my loved one with a calm and happy face.

Homeward Bound . . .

The City streets are dark with crowds – a moving, surging throng.
All rushing, jostling eagerly, they press their way along . . .
And east and west and north and south from out the City's heart,
a million wheels are turning round, tubes, trains, trams – all a part.

Of one great movement, streaming out, the countless faces blend
in one vast sea, yet each is turned towards its journey's end . . .
A single purpose drives them on – they meet on common ground,
united in the urge for flight . . . The workers homeward bound.

Home

I try to make my home a place that's beautiful to see,
to fill each room with lovely things – and perfect harmony,
to polish up the copper pots, the silver and the brass,
and rub the walnut table till it gleams like crystal glass . . .
But home is not mere furniture.
The objects we see here are visible expressions of a wonderful
Idea –
a power that draws with ties of love wherever we may roam.
The centre of the universe and of the heart – the Home.

Tea-Time

I've invited my very best friend round to tea,
so the cakes must be golden and light . . .
I must see that there's plenty of fresh currant bread –
everything must be perfect, just right.
I shall use the blue china – the old willow set,
and the cloth with the ivory lace.
I shall put the chairs ready a whole hour before
and be waiting for her – in my place.
And my day will be full of excitement and fun,
but I know when it comes to an end,
there'll be only one memory left in my mind –
taking tea with my very best friend.

Grandfather Clock

There's a grandfather clock in the quiet old hall,
and it strikes with a deep-throated chime.
For he booms out the hours with a terrible voice,
and he cuts up our lives into Time.

He's a century old and he looks with disdain
on the folks who stare into his face.
For he knows that when their little lives flicker out,
he'll be still standing there in his place . . .

And he whirrs and he chuckles deep down in his works,
for he knows that we're all in his power
as, relentless, he roars out his challenge to men,
and he can't take back one single hour.

Gifts

Let us give and give again of all that we possess.
Not from the purse but from the heart – bright smiles and
                                                    kindliness,
the helping hand, the loving thought, the friendly word of praise,
encouraging some lonely soul through dark and stormy days . . .
The very poorest may be lavish with these lovely gifts.
Without a penny we may give the kindness that uplifts.
God never stints – He gives to men His riches from above.
Then may we give abundantly, the good gift of our love.

Listen!

'Listen' – that's a lovely word – it makes us quiet and still.
There's so much in the world to hear: the birds that chirp and trill;
the wild wind fluting in the trees; the drumming of the rain
the muffled fluttering of moths against a window pane:
Chopin, Beethoven, Liszt and Grieg – giants of music's art
created golden melodies to stir the human heart.

The world is full of lovely sounds – they fall about our ears.
Remembered in serenity, they echo down the years:
a voice we loved, a waterfall, a violin, a thrush,
all steal into the quiet heart in Memory's solemn hush . . .
So close your eyes and listen, you will hear all kinds of things –
the secret language of the flowers, the whirr of fairies' wings . . .

Shopping

It's fun to go shopping with someone you like –
some good friend who won't mind if you stop,
and you gaze in the windows and wander about
looking round in each different shop . . .

It's so nice just to stare at the things that you'd like,
though you haven't the money to buy –
pretty hats, shoes and gowns, books and furniture too,
lovely pictures – you have to pass by!

But I'm sure I'd be bored if I had all these things
for myself, heaps of money to spend,
for the wishing and wanting is half of the fun
of a day round the shops with a friend.

Fireside

The chairs are drawn around the fire – we gather round the blaze,
united in the fireside circle of the winter days.
The lamp is lit, the curtains drawn – and yet it's incomplete,
because the firelight shadows fall upon an empty seat . . .

Oh, please God, pity those who sit and face a vacant chair,
remembering the happy face – the loved one laughing there.
May He uplift them, give them strength to play their separate parts
and send His warmth to melt the frozen winter in their hearts . . .
Oh, may they feel the unseen presence of the one that's gone,
inspiring them with courage to be brave and carry on.

Broken Romance

You told me your story – a picture in words;
a garden with roses and sweet-singing birds;
and two lovers dreaming the moments away,
bewitched by the spell of the blue Summer's day . . .
A brief hour of magic and Love's ecstasies –
now locked in the casket of old memories.
The Summer has ended, the roses have gone,
the lovers have parted, yet Love lingers on.
The songs and the laughter have ended in tears,
as lonely, heartbroken they face the long years . . .
A sad little story, but who knows, my friend?
Your romance may still have a beautiful end.

Letters

The telephone has almost killed the sweet and gentle art
of writing lengthy letters, friend to friend, and heart to heart.
For people haven't got the time in this speed-crazy day
to put their thoughts on paper in a lovely, charming way . . .
To draw from wells of quiet thought, and set oneself apart,
to write a long, long letter from the fullness of the heart . . .
To take the pen and wander on down Memory's fragrant way,
reviving all the golden dreams of some sweet yesterday . . .

And so I keep my letters, tattered pages from the years.
They weave the story of the past with laughter, hope and tears.
They bridge the gulf from heart to heart. I read them all again,
and catch the quiet echoes of the rapture and the pain.

From a Window

The people who sit at a window and watch
as the crowds in the street pass along
see more than the people who rush to and fro
taking part in the big, noisy throng.
They get the best view of the things that occur
from the quiet of their hidden retreat,
while the folks who go pushing and jostling along
only see their small bit of the street . . .

It's the same in the swirl and chaos of life
when your world seems all frenzy and din –
just withdraw, and go into your own secret self;
looking out from the window within,
you will find that your troubles diminish and fade,
as remote as the far stars on high,
then serene in the stillness, your heart will grow wise
as you watch the mad world rushing by.

Cradles

I love to look at cradles, for they seem to symbolise
the whole of human tenderness; their pretty frills and ties
are emblems of the love that spreads its kind protective wings
around the helpless and the weak, and small defenceless things . . .
And we are all defenceless from the moment of our birth –
frail, tiny figures strutting on our little spinning earth.
Our world is whirling in the void, we face Eternity –
We cannot probe the secrets of our hidden Destiny . . .

And yet we, too, are cradles, safe within His tender care.
The Love too deep for man to know is always waiting there –
creating, and controlling, suns and stars and worlds above.
And we are safe within the cradle of that perfect Love . . .

Slippers

I love to see a pair of slippers on the fireside mat.
It looks untidy, I'll admit, but who cares about that?
For slippers are so intimate, so nice and homely too,
especially when they're very old – I hate them when they're new!.

They seem to know they're waiting for two tired and weary feet.
I'm sure they hear their owners coming homeward down the
street . . .

Our shoes may look quite trim and smart as we go on our way,
but when we sit beside the fire and dream at close of day,
it's nice to take them off and slip our slippers on instead
– and let them take us quietly up the stairs, and so to bed.

Bedside Books

My house is full of well-loved books. They're scattered round
    the place –
in unexpected corners, on the shelves and in the case.
But on the table by my bed, I keep a little row
of precious books – my favourite ones – and when I'm tired I go
and find some passage that inspires with words like angel wings
that lift me up above the swirl of petty human things . . .
A truth from some great poet's pen, a lovely, lilting phrase –
a message that will spur me on, and light the darkest days.

Goodnight, Children

Goodnight, children! – and dream your happy dreams.
Forget your cares, forget your tears, and all your gallant schemes.
Tomorrow lies before you like an undiscovered land,
with shining possibilities – the lovely things you've planned
are blurred into a golden haze in which you play your part
in valiant adventures with a brave and fearless heart.

The rabbit and the kittens and the fishes in the streams,
the soldiers and the sugar mouse go marching through your dreams.
And though the darkness must descend, and toys be put away,
God always sends Tomorrow when He takes away Today.

Welcome

'Welcome' is a lovely word. It means so many things –
the warmth of human friendship and the pleasure that it brings;
true greetings of the kindly hearts who share what they possess;
the cheery hearth, the cosy home – and joy and happiness . . .
For hospitality does not depend upon our store.
It's what we mean by 'Welcome' when our friends are at the door.

The Spare Room

It's only just a little room with simple, homely things.
The only sound comes from the eaves, the sound of tiny wings.
The boards are stained a shining brown, the walls are painted
cream –
a simple room, a quiet room, in which to sleep and dream . . .

I like to peep inside the door and take it unawares,
to see the oaken bedstead and the little wicker chairs.
And then, in some mysterious way, I feel the room is blessed.
Whoever sleeps within its walls will find a perfect rest.

It offers to the restless heart a hospitality
that's warm and rich because it springs from real simplicity.

And in this humble little room its meaning is expressed –
the blessing of the presence of the well-beloved guest.

Roofs

I love to climb the hill that lies behind our little town.
And when the sun shines after rain, it's lovely to look down
upon the little coloured roofs, lit by the sun's bright ray –
a beautiful mosaic, brown and red and green and grey . . .

The town looks small and toy-like underneath the sky's great dome;
and as I gaze, I realise that each roof is a home
where people strive and work and play, and children laugh and cry,
and men and women play their parts, and live and love and die . . .

And yet the town looks so content, so happy and serene,
with all its little shining roofs of red and brown and green.
And as the daylight fades to dusk, I watch as sunset gleams,
and pray God sends to every home joy, peace, and happy dreams.

Sleep

Sleep is a soft and gentle hand that charms away all strife,
and draws us with a magic touch from out the grasp of Life.
It throws into our tired eyes, the golden dust of dreams.
And we forget our failures and our little futile schemes . . .

If you've a grievance in your heart, don't rail and storm and weep,
just put a finger on the lips and then lie down and sleep.
And in the morning when you wake, you'll take a different view –
for God gives you another day in which to start anew.

Alarm-Clock

When we are sleeping in our beds, the grim, relentless clock
starts ringing loudly in our ears and gives us such a shock.
It says, 'Come on, you lazy thing, and don't you hesitate.
There's work to do, you know the time, so don't dare be late!'

Oh, how we hate that cruel clock, especially when we're cold.
We have to leave our cosy beds and do just as we're told,
and face the bleak realities that crowd upon the mind –
begin the day and leave our rosy dreamland far behind.

And Life's like that – we think that we're secure and safe and warm
and suddenly we find we've got to face the strife and storm.
Some trouble comes along and gives us such a nasty knock.
Just like the rude awakening of that fiendish thing – the Clock!

Jealousy

He looks at Baby Peter with his sad and mournful eyes.
He doesn't understand things, and his thoughts he can't disguise.
He used to be the petted darling of the family,
and now he takes a second place – that's plain enough to see!
For years he was their own devoted pal, and then one day
a tiny stranger came to town. Imagine his dismay!
His master and his mistress did their best to make amends,
and show him that the four of them could be the greatest friends.

He wags his tail and gives a sniff and tries to raise a smile,
although his faithful doggie heart is breaking all the while,
because he knows that things can never never be the same.
The world is turned all upside down – since Baby Peter came.

Potpourri

Pretty painted china bowl upon the window sill –
I love to catch the sweet elusive perfume you distil.
It steals upon me in the greyness of the twilight hours –
the half-forgotten fragrance of the lovely summer flowers . . .

I close my eyes, and when this sweetness hangs upon the air,
the winter scene is blotted out – I see a garden fair,
with roses, pinks and lavender, with mignonette and musk,
and all the beauty of a garden in a summer dusk . . .

I wish I could preserve my happy memories like this –
the dreams of youth, the golden hopes, the hours of perfect bliss.
All gathered up like petals, stored away, and set apart,
hidden in the secret places of a quiet heart.

Old Age

Old Age never comes to us when Youth is in the mind.
When we have left the wild, ecstatic days of Spring behind,
we come upon a richer time of deep content and peace,
when all the heart's red wounds are healed, and our rebellions
                                    cease . . .
When quiet hours bring memories that steal from out the years –
and lift us up on wings of dreams, and sorrow disappears.
And only happiness remains from all the crowded past,
if we have gathered to ourselves the things that really last.

The body may be broken, but the mind may still expand
and touch the rosy fringes of that good and better Land . . .
The spirit is forever young. Unfettered it can rise
and probe the secrets of the wind, the stars, the trees, the skies . . .
The old may go adventuring to seek the heart's desire
and live a thousand lives again when dreaming by the fire.

Happy Trio

Baby, Mother, Grandmamma – the trio is complete.
Three happy people. Life for them is good and very sweet.
For Grandma finds fulfilment in her daughter's perfect joy.
And mother has her first-born child – a little baby boy . . .

Oh, may the years be very kind, no tears and fears and frowns.
Yet changes come, babies grow up. Life is all ups and downs.
But may you cling together as you go the winding way –
and be a happy little trio, as you are today.

Happy Home

I read your note, my friend, and I can picture where you live.
A happy home – what more on earth can God in heaven give?
A cottage nestling in the trees, a place of peace and rest,
made perfect by a love that's true – our home is surely blessed . . .

I see the red brick fireplace, and the brass all shining bright.
I see the pretty curtains that you draw in every night.
Oh may you keep it as it is – paradise for two,
where fondest hopes are satisfied, and all your dreams come true.

Home Sweet Home

Home may be a castle or a villa or a cot.
No matter if it's grand or small – it is a sacred spot,
where we can come when we are tired of Life's mad circus show,
of shams and empty pleasures blindly rushing to and fro.
And seeking for the happiness that Home alone can give,
God give us quiet and simple hearts and teach us how to live!

A home may be an anchor in the troubled storms of life,
a refuge from this world of pain and selfishness and strife . . .
To welcome us at any time wherever we may roam –
four walls around a universe that men call Home Sweet Home.

Pie-Crust

Pie-crust looks so nice and firm, and yet it always breaks.
It's made just to be crumbled into little bits and flakes.
And oh, how many promises are broken in this way –
made in an idle moment, and forgotten the next day!
Think well before you make a promise. Keep it if you do,
or you will find that people will lose confidence in you.
Somebody counts upon your word, so don't betray their trust.
A promise is a promise, not a little bit of crust . . .
Why wait until tomorrow? Now's the time – don't be deterred.
In big things or in trifles – we must keep our word.

Christening

'What shall we call him?' Mother asked. 'The christening's today.
We must make up our minds – I really don't know what to say . . .
The aunties and the uncles will be here at half-past three.
And Father's name must come into it – whatever shall it be?

Patrick, David, Stephen, John – they're all so very nice.
If only he could speak to us and give us his advice!
No matter what our choice may be, God bless my baby's name.
And though it may not bring us glory, wealth or worldly fame,
oh, may it be remembered for the things of highest worth –
for all the splendid things that really matter on this earth –

straight dealing and good sportsmanship, high standards and fair
                                                                    play:
the name that we shall give our little baby boy today
. . . A name to honour and respect, and when Life's shadows fall,
he'll realise a good name is the greatest thing of all.'

Cottage Garden

What could be more lovely on a golden summer day
than this old cottage garden somewhere Surrey way.
Lupins like bright candles burning in the sultry air.
Poppies like red wisps of paper in the sun's fierce glare.
Pansies dreaming by the borders – wide-eyed, in a trance.
Boughs of apple shuffling shadows where the sunbeams dance.
Butterflies with powdered wings and drowsy droning bees.
Scent of full-blown cabbage roses drifting on the breeze.
Passionflowers that fall across the lattice in a shower.
Who am I, dear God, that I should have this perfect hour?

Decisions

We reach the parting of the ways, and then we must decide
which pathway we shall take – it's hard, we have no human guide.
Each road is dark and unexplored. We face the great unknown –
and in that final moment everyone must stand alone . . .

So much may hang upon a word. So many things at stake –
careers, and lives and happiness, and in the choice we make
we spin the webs of destiny for good or ill. And so
when you're perplexed and cannot see the way in which to go,

be still and wait for guidance and you will not wait in vain –
no need for panic or distress, no need to strive and strain . . .
Trust with a quiet confidence. You'll know the thing to do,
and you will hear the voice of Wisdom at the heart of you.

Homecoming

Coming home – the very words turn grey skies into blue.
Coming home . . . O happy thought! For life begins anew.
Hands stretched out in welcome from the homely little door,
things in their accustomed place, just as they were before.
Tables, carpets, books and chairs all smile as if they knew
that Mother's coming home today. They share the secret too.

It's lonely in the dear old home without her smiling face.
Her absence makes it seem a very dreary kind of place.
But now the longed-for day has come. She's coming home again –
forgotten all the anxious hours of worry and of pain . . .
God bless the sweet reunion of this happy family –
and grant Thy peace and happiness through all the years to be.

Long-Distance Call

A voice was borne across the sea
to greet a happy family;
imagine their surprise when they
could hear their loved one far away . . .
The dear familiar voice came through,
reviving memories anew,
and they'll recall in years to be
that voice across the distant sea.

This is the wonder of our day –
that from a thousand miles away
a voice could travel on a beam.
It's like the magic of a dream!
It brings our friends back home again,
without the aid of ship or train.
It brings them close, though seas divide –
it is as if they're at our side . . .
The lonely hours have never been.
A voice can bridge the years between.
Goodbye is robbed of all its pain.
It's so long – till we phone again.

Lovers' Lane

It's lovely in the summer days – a perfect lovers' lane.
It's shady in the sunshine and it's fragrant in the rain;
the wild flowers in the hedges fling their perfume on the breeze.
From dawn to dusk the birds trill out their music in the trees . . .
When day is ended and the world is wrapped in evening's calm,
the lovers down the leafy lane go strolling arm in arm;
they dream Love's gay romantic dreams, exploring magic realms,
until the moon comes peeping through the tangle of the elms . . .

Then homeward to the village where the lighted windows gleam,
enchanted in the secret rapture of a lover's dream . . .
What ardent hopes are harboured in the heart of man and maid!
The common earth is holy ground when, brave and unafraid,
they view from youth's high peak of faith the years that are to be –
and heart to heart they make their vows for all Eternity . . .

Oh, may they never lose this sense of magic and delight
that clings about them as they walk, enraptured, through the night.
No matter what the years may hold of pleasure or of pain,
may life for them be one long stroll along lover's lane.

Picnic

It's fun to have a picnic on a lovely summer's day
in some green meadow where a little river winds its way;
a fragrant bank where willows trail their branches gracefully.
It's nice to have a party underneath a kind old tree . . .
To spread the cloth upon the grass, and set the plates around;
to drink your tea and eat your cakes while seated on the ground –
fat doughnuts, jam and creamy buns, and things that normally
you really wouldn't dream of eating with your cup of tea!
Your fingers may be sticky, but that's half the fun of it,
the wasps may settle in the jam, but you won't care a bit!

But when you've had your picnic, don't forget to make the place
exactly as you found it, leaving not a single trace . . .
For if, for instance, you were asked to tea with friends next door –
you wouldn't leave a lot of litter lying on the floor,
now would you? And it's just the same in Nature's lovely bowers.
She's so hospitable and kind – she gives us fields and flowers,
and shady nooks by babbling brooks, where we can take our ease,
and have a picnic underneath the shelter of the trees.

Reliability

When you make a promise, keep it, trifling though it be.
Win a reputation for reliability.
Never go back on your word or disappoint your friends.
Don't do something mean and weak, then rush to make amends.

Can you be relied upon to carry through a plan?
Can you be relied upon to do the best you can?
Are you to be trusted in some great emergency?
Can you take the weight of a responsibility?

Fickle folks draw fickle friends, and many friends mean none.
In this world we're truly lucky if we find but one.
One faithful friend that needs no vow, no gift, no bribe, no tie.
One true and dear and trusted friend on whom we may rely . . .

And such a friend comes not by chance. Life's laws are good
and just,
for friendship such as this is built on honour, faith and trust.

Birthday Flowers

Whether your birthday season comes
    with autumn's rich chrysanthemums,
or with the winter's frosty air
    when blooms are scarce and flowers are rare,
or if your introduction here
    was in the springtime of the year,
your favourites are those, I'd say,
    which greet you on your natal day,
saying, Many happy hours,
    in the language of the flowers.

Time

Life's a gamble. Life's a scramble. Fret and turmoil, strife and noise.
Life's a worry. What's the hurry? Give me peace and quiet joys.

Life's all clamour; fake and glamour, tinsel shams and vulgar show;
fight for money. Aren't folks funny? Rushing madly to and fro.

Give me leisure; simple pleasure; time in which to stand and stare.
Time to wonder; time to wander; time to dream; and time to spare.
Time for gazing; time for raising weary eyes to leaf and wing;
time for praying; time for saying: Thank You, God, for everything.

The Happy Day

Let this be a happy day –
all the while and all the way.
May the dearest dream come true,
and the best be granted you . . .
Good friends to your door be sent,
and your heart be well content
with what the day may leave behind.
Time be good and Life be kind.

Life's the Thing

Life's the thing – so be alive and always look alive,
whether you are seventeen or rising seventy-five.
It's not the length of years that counts; it is the quality
that determines what kind of a living yours is going to be . . .
There's no generation gap. Age is illusory.
Life's the thing. Enjoy it, love it, live it gloriously.

Bereavement

Sorrow comes unto the door of every family.
Changes come as loved ones go. That's life. It has to be . . .
The empty future looms ahead. A blank we have to face.
In the heart there is a silence and a vacant place.

Death breaks up the old familiar pattern of the days.
We have to work a new one out in unaccustomed ways.
At first it seems impossible, but when we've dried our tears
we see another pattern being traced out through the years.

Content

Content I pray I'll always be
with home and hearth and family . . .
Content in my small realm to reign.
Happy in my own domain.

Thankful for whatever's there,
though it be but frugal fare . . .
Every meal a sacrament
when the spirit is content.

Content with what comes to my door.
Not always wanting something more.
But grateful for the odds and ends
that a God of mercy sends.

When Troubles Come

When troubles come we find our truest friends.
The knowledge of their affection lends
a glow to gloom, a cheering, warming ray
that helps us face the darkness of the day.

The word that heartens and the kindly thought
give us courage, comfort and support . . .
If we have proved a friend to somebody,
we too find friendship in adversity.

Something That Belonged to Mother

Often when I'm looking for a thing I have mislaid,
I come on some forgotten odds and ends. Time seems to fade,
and in a flash leap across the years because I see
things that stab my heart awake with Mother's memory.

A photograph, some beads, a thimble, kept I know not why –
a sentimental whim has always made me put them by;
and so they keep on turning up to haunt me through the years.
It's foolish, but I cling to them – these little souvenirs.

This Lovely Memory

Dear, let us remember this when we are tired and old –
When we sit beside the fire and days are drear and cold.
Let us warm our hearts against this lovely memory –
keeping it forever bright through all the years to be.
Drifting on the river in a dream world of our own;
gliding through enchanted country, you and I alone . . .
Sunlit waters rippling by and willows up above –
two young people whispering the old, old words of love.

Say you never will forget this golden afternoon.
Time will bring its changes and the winter comes too soon . . .
Say you will remember when the gold has turned to grey –
Let us keep unto the end the dream we've dreamed today.

Just Kindness

Kindness, just kindness is all that it takes
to make a day happy, for kindliness makes
for peace and for cheerfulness, grace and goodwill,
stirring no trouble, and speaking no ill.

Feeling for others and trying to ease
the burden that presses, to help and to please;
forgetting yourself and your own heavy load;
thinking of somebody else on the road.

The value of kindness you cannot assess.
Spoken or written no word can express
how one little kindness can make someone's day –
giving him courage to go on his way,
a smile on his lips and a song in his mind,
just because somebody somewhere was kind.

Give Me the Simple Things of Life

Give me the simple things of life: a cottage hearth, a quiet room,
a little garden green with trees, where birds make song midst leaf
    and bloom.

Give me the happy things of life: a heart that's merry all the way,
an outlook that is broad and bright, a spirit that is brave and gay.

Give me the lasting things of life: a faith that nothing can destroy –
the kindly company of friends, and love to crown my days with joy.

Time Alone

Time alone can make a garden, giving it the mellow tones
of the lichen and the moss that stain the worn and weathered
stones . . .
Only old well-rooted trees can spread their branches thick and
wide,
casting long and lovely shadows on the lawns at eventide.

Man can plan and plant and work it – but it is the years that bring
growth and glory in their train and leave their mark on everything.
Time alone can give that touch that makes a garden fair to see,
rounding off the edges with the beauty of maturity.

The Blessing

The blessing of a loving mother nobody can measure.
You cannot put it into words or price this precious treasure . . .
She suffers when you suffer and she shares in your success.
She works for you and wishes for your health and happiness.

Your love express in words before she passes on her way –
then there'll be no sadness over what you failed to say . . .
It is now that kindness counts; we sometimes leave too late
a thank you for some little thing that we appreciate.

Always Young

I'm always young while you are here.
You are my childhood, mother dear.
You are my youth. Your smiling face
comes haunting every secret place
within the caves of memory;
for you were always there with me
in all those wonderful events
of the years of innocence
when the sun shone every day.
Or so it seemed; all fun and play.
Life was one long lovely Spring.
There was a bloom on everything.

While you're still near I catch the glow
reflected from the long ago.
Stay, dear Mother. Never go.

Mother of the Bride

She has played her part and now there's nothing to be done –
but play the charming hostess with a smile for everyone . . .
There she is, a radiant figure, elegant and smart,
although we know just how she must be feeling in her heart.

For her, as well as for her girl, it is the day of days.
She knows it is a milestone and the ending of a phase.
But ends are new beginnings where the roads of life divide.
So Time be kind, and may God bless the Mother of the bride.

Happy Morning

Greet the day with happy heart and vow that it will be
a well-lived and a worthwhile day. Accept it gratefully
as a good and precious gift, a newly given chance
to wrest a blessing out of every twist of circumstance.

Grey the day may look to you when first you wake to it.
Don't go by appearance. Later on it may be lit
with sunny gleams and golden dreams, adventure and romance.
You must not judge a day by what it looks like at a glance.

Even though the day holds out no hope of happiness,
don't despise it or despair for you can never guess
what it may unfold before the sunset dies away.
Greet with glad thanksgiving the beginning of each day.

Make a Rainbow

If your world looks gloomy and you're feeling grim and glum,
make a rainbow for yourself, don't wait for one to come.
Don't sit watching at the window for the clouds to part.
There'll soon be a rainbow if you start one in your heart.

Take some lovely thought out of a poem or a prayer.
Turn it over in your mind and let it linger there.
Keep out every memory that dims the light within,
and hold on to the magic word that lets the brightness in.

Work your own small miracle and make the dull days glow.
Put some sunshine into life and let the glory show.
Make a rainbow for yourself with colours brave and gay,
and underneath its golden arch your cares will fade away.

Our Dancing Years

It is only a melody recalled from long ago,
but it has the power to set my empty heart aglow
with memories that go back to the rich romantic past,
when love was new and life was good; so good – too good to last.

It is only a melody upon a record played,
but it fills the room with pictures that can never fade,
more vivid and more real than those that hang upon the wall.
How wonderful that this small disc can resurrect it all
with such a deep intensity,
and bring you laughing back to me
without the hurt, without the tears,
to live again our dancing years.

Too Late Now

When you come we meet as friends, but when you say goodbye,
you leave a haunting sadness like the echo of a sigh . . .
Merry is the laughter, gay the talk and bright the scene,
but underneath it all I hear the words: it might have been.

Yes, indeed, it might have been. I see it in your eyes.
We might have loved each other once – but things went otherwise.
Life works out its own designs, and we survive somehow.
All is for the best, they say. Too late for loving now . . .
Too late for disentangling the frayed and twisted thread;
too late to obliterate the foolish words we said.
For a different kind of life the stage has now been set.
Burden not the present with the ashes of regret.

Gardens Bring Back Memories

Gardens bring back memories, the thought of bygone hours
mingles with the present as you walk amongst your flowers . . .
They stir the recollection of some unforgotten place,
and call to mind out of the past, a scene, a voice, a face.

Even when the last rose falls upon the frosted clay,
you catch upon the wintry wind a song of yesterday.
In every corner of the garden something you will see
that evokes within your heart some lovely memory.

Time Will Bring It Back

No good deed is ever wasted and no kind word said in vain
for the good we do for others, life brings back to us again . . .
Every seed of love you sow will spring up somewhere on the road,
and the sacrifice you make will serve to lighten someone's load.

No good deed is lost to God although it may be lost to view.
Cast your bread upon the waters. Time will bring it back to you.

A Window Looking West

I love a room that has a window looking to the west.
Morning has its glories, but it's this I love the best:
the evening view that opens at the gold end of the day,
when the sun goes down in pearly clouds of rose and grey.

At the day's beginning sunny windows we must shun.
Life comes rushing in and there are duties to be done . . .
No one has the time to sit and watch the spectacle
of the dawn that makes the world all fresh and beautiful.

But when the doors are closed upon the busy crowded days,
it is good to have a room where you can turn your gaze
to the quiet landscapes of the view you love the best
through the golden casements of a window looking west.

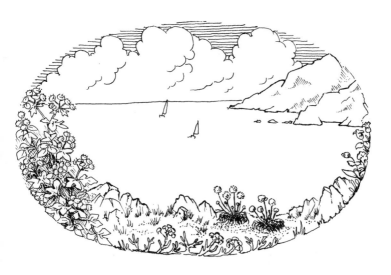

Lose Yourself

Lose yourself with all your wants, your worry and your woe.
Lose yourself in other people's troubles. Yours will go . . .
Lose yourself by getting lost in someone else's maze –
helping one another through the dark unhappy days.

Lose yourself in something bigger than your own affairs.
Lose yourself, immersed in all the problems and the cares
that surround you day by day. You'll soon forget your own –
for you'll come to realise that you are not alone,
suffering in isolation; others suffer too.
Lose yourself to find yourself and when at last you do,
you will find a better person than you were before,
when you lived for self alone behind your own front door.

Not Easy

It's not always easy to hold your tongue when people are unkind.
It's not always easy to walk away and put it from your mind –
but quarrelling never put anything right, it seems to make things
    worse,
and leaves you with a hornet's nest of grievances to nurse.

It's not always easy to turn aside and show the other cheek,
because you're afraid they will think that you are spiritless and
    weak . . .
No, it's not easy but it's the only thing to do you'll find –
if you want to keep your friendships and your peace of mind.

A Friend

A friend is someone who will always try to understand,
one in whom you can confide when things get out of hand . . .
Someone who will listen when by bad luck you've been hit,
never offering advice unless you ask for it.

So grapple him, said Shakespeare, to your heart with hoops of
    steel.
Lonely you will never be and helpless never feel,
if you have a friend like this when crosses you must bear.
You may not meet for months, but when he's needed . . . he'll
    be there.

I Walked in Memory Lane Today

I walked in Memory Lane today.
It was roses all the way,
until I heard a voice that said:
Turn back. Walk not the path ahead.

But on I pressed till suddenly
thorns and nettles tortured me . . .
My fingers bled, my sleeve was rent,
as down the tangled track I went.

Go not too often or too far
along the road where memories are,
but find content and pleasures new
in what the present holds for you.

Take What Comes

Don't expect perfection for you'll never find it here.
This is earth, not heaven, so with charity and cheer
take what comes – the good, the bad, and don't start whimpering
when you're disappointed with a person or a thing.

Do not worship idols and complain when you have found
feet of clay beneath the robes in which you've wrapped them
                                        round . . .
Everyone is human. Do not be too critical
when someone fails, Remember that you, too, are fallible.

Keep your ideals in your heart and set your standard high,
but don't lose faith when things go wrong. Just let the storm
                                        blow by . . .
Do not ask too much of life or reach beyond your range.
Accept and learn to live content with what you cannot change.

One by One

You do not have to take in one great stride
the busy day that lies ahead of you.
When troubles loom around on every side,
and nowhere can you see a clear way through.
Just take it step by step and you will find
fears fade like snowflakes melting in the sun . . .
The worst things happen only in the mind,
and problems are disposed of one by one.

So Little

The gentle smile, the reconciling touch
can cost so little and can mean so much –
to heal a breach or mend a friendship broken,
a letter written, or a sentence spoken.

What hurts and pangs we suffer needlessly!
What pains inflict, because we cannot see
how much we lost through conflicts and contentions,
poisoning life with quarrels and dissensions.

Let them all go and love triumphant be
over all evil, hate, greed, jealousy . . .
Love's tender word, forbearing and forgiving,
brings to the heart true peace and joy of living.

Cosiness

Some folks yearn for luxury, for grand and costly things –
but I prefer the homely touch; a cosy room that brings
a warming glow into the heart, a room that seems to say,
'Come right in and welcome,' on a cold and gloomy day.

These are the things that give a place a snug and friendly air:
the gleam of oak and brass and copper and a chintzy chair.
A bowl of flowers, a shelf of books, a softly shaded light.
And a little casement hung with curtains gay and bright.

A firelit ingle and a kettle singing merrily.
A pile of logs upon the hearth – the table set for tea.
Who would wish for what is showy and magnificent?
These are the things that make for comfort and for sweet content.

The Instrument

Play life like an instrument, making melodies.
Change the daily discords into harmonies . . .
Draw the sweetness from it. Somebody may hear
the tune behind the strident sounds that jar upon the ear.
Make your music as you move through the world's distress.
Someone passing by may catch your note of happiness . . .
Play life gently, play it softly. Play with style and grace –
bringing beauty out of what is dull and commonplace.

Happiness Waiting for You

There is light at the end of the tunnel.
There is calm at the end of the storm . . .
There is rest at the end of the journey,
and a hearth that is welcome and warm.

There's a star on the top of the mountain
you can touch when the last crag is scaled.
There's a certain reward for the faithful
at the point where they think they have failed.

There's a spring at the end of the winter
and behind the black cloud it is blue . . .
There's a song at the heart of your sorrow,
and happiness waiting for you.

Give Your Love

Give your love to others. Don't spend it on yourself.
Give your heart's good treasure. Don't hoard it on the shelf . . .
Give a word of comfort. Give a helping hand.
Give where it is needed. Try to understand.

Give the best that's in you to the job you do.
Give the world your blessing and it blesses you . . .
Give your life to something that is well worthwhile.
Give – and never ever forget to give a smile.

The Best in Life

The best and sweetest things in life are things you cannot buy:
the music of the birds at dawn, the rainbows in the sky;
the dazzling magic of the stars, the miracle of light;
the precious gifts of health and strength, of hearing, speech and
sight;

the peace of mind that crowns a busy
life of work well done; a faith in God
that deepens as you face the setting sun;
the pearl of love, the gems of friendship.
As the years go by
you find the greatest blessings are the things you cannot buy.

If the Heart Is Singing

If the heart is singing you cannot go far wrong –
for you will discover there's magic in a song
that scares away the demons that throng around us all,
wanting us to stumble and to see us fall.

If the heart is singing nothing can get through –
only that which strengthens and what is best for you.

Let the world go grumbling and grinding on its way,
for you'll have the secret that lights the common day.
You'll see the hidden glory behind the leaden cloud.
Lightly you will travel, head high and back unbowed,
for when the heart is singing the soul is singing too.
Your sins will be forgiven, for every day is new.

As Roses Have Thorns

As roses have thorns, so does love have its times
    of testings, frustrations and pains.
But what is it worth if it cannot withstand
    the pressures, the heartaches and strains?

Love's depths can't be measured by kiss, word or gift –
    but by sympathy tender and true;
the will to forbear, to forgive,
to forget, and to take the most generous view –
hiding the scars and the stings that still smart,
ready to laugh and to make a new start.

Happy House

Is this a happy house? Yes. You will know
once you have stepped inside. Faces will show
that sort of happiness none can disguise.
It's in the smile of the lips and the eyes.

Is this a happy house? Yes, if Love here
makes its abiding and dwells year by year . . .
Love's quiet presence is sensed and is heard
in helpfulness, kindness and courteous words.

Is this a happy house? Yes, if so be –
somebody prays in it. Prayer secretly
sweetens and brightens wherever it's said,
and calls down a blessing on every head.

The Haven of the Heart

I never cease to find it strange
how in a flash the world can change . . .
Things can happen overnight,
and suddenly it all comes right.

Life may not go the way you planned.
You cannot hope to understand the hidden hand
of Providence
that works unseen behind events.
But patience waits to serve her turn,
and if on faith you lean, you learn
to live by truths not understood,
that lead at last unto the good
that you have sought unconsciously;
the haven where your heart would be.

Somebody's Tomorrow

Is anyone the happier for meeting you today?
Has anyone been prayed for just because he came your way?
Has anyone been helped because you stopped to lend a hand,
spared a little time to listen, tried to understand?

Has anyone been made to feel that God was somewhere near?
Has someone somewhere been relieved of worry and of fear?
Has someone rediscovered faith in what is good and true –
seen another side to life, another point of view?

If the answer's Yes, then you have earned your night's repose.
If no, your day was wasted, spent in vain, and at its close
there can be no satisfaction; not unless you say
that somebody's tomorrow will be better than today.

Together Again

Now we're together once more, we two.
The past we will bury and start anew,
making the best of what years remain,
mending our marriage, beginning again.

Wiser for every mistake we made,
letting unhappy memories fade,
thankful for having this second chance
to pick up the threads of the old romance.

Forward we'll look to the days ahead,
forgetting the things we did and said.
So foolish! Now everything's marvellous.
The future is ours and it's up to us.

A Promise

Keep a promise to a child whatever it may be.
Never ever break your word, but keep it faithfully . . .
Disappointments hurt the children, giving needless pain.
Once you let them down they won't believe in you again.

If you want your children to be honest, straight and true,
never give them cause to lose their confidence in you.
Set them an example. Always stand by what you've said.
Don't sow doubts or start suspicions in a little head.

Children have long memories. They bank on what you say.
Don't raise hopes then dash them with the words, 'Some other day'.
Once you've made a promise let them see that you are tied.
Teach them that it's something that you must not set aside.

Heart or Head

My heart is saying: This is love. But can it really be?
My heart is saying: This is it. It says you're meant for me . . .
But how, I wonder, can I tell if this is truly so.
Can the wayward heart be trusted? How am I to know?

Common sense says: Wait awhile. Don't risk a big mistake.
Pause before you start to think about a wedding cake . . .
Look before you take a final leap into the blue.
But my heart says, 'Fiddlesticks!' So what am I to do?

I admit that in the past I've often been misled.
But now it comes to this: am I to follow heart or head?
I ought to heed the voice that says it can't be genuine,
and yet I have a feeling that my heart is going to win.

Let Love Speak

Let the word of peace be spoken,
when relationships are broken.
Let Love speak and heal the smart
of wounds inflicted on the heart.

Let Love's language, sweet and tender,
its own gentle service render –
saying what is kind and wise,
with the lips or with the eyes.

Let no grievance leave an ember
that perhaps you may remember,
and regret in later years,
with your penitential tears.

Try forgiving. Try confessing.
Let Love speak the final blessing,
casting every doubt away,
before the closing of the day.

Ideal Home

It doesn't have to have the latest kitchen gadgetry,
central heating or a fridge. Nor does it need to be
like an illustration in a glossy magazine,
all complete with television and a wash-machine.

You can have the ideal home without these odds and ends,
if you have the things on which true happiness depends:
the comfort and companionship of friends and family,
centred round a hearth where there is peace and harmony.

These things make the ideal home and work the miracle.
The touch that turns the commonplace into the beautiful.
The love that lights the daily round and brightens every part.
The sunshine of good humour and the kindness of the heart.

Boy & Girl Affair

When you fall in love around the age of seventeen,
everything looks wonderful and wears a rosy sheen . . .
It's as if you're in a bubble floating through the clouds,
drifting in a rainbow-world away above the crowds.

It seldom lasts, that first romance . . . but treat it tenderly:
this morning madness of the heart, this April ecstasy . . .
This Springtime of experience when life is fresh and sweet
that comes upon you unawares and sweeps you off your feet.

Years will pass and it will be forgotten utterly –
then some day, one day, something will revive the memory,
like a sudden breath of blossoms on the wintry air,
and you'll remember once again that boy and girl affair.

Condolence

A few brief words I'm sending you in all sincerity,
to assure you of my deep and heartfelt sympathy . . .
When sorrows come to those we love we know not what to say,
words are so inadequate our feelings to convey.

None can really share our griefs. We suffer each apart,
for only God can speak the word that mends a broken heart.
Only He can give the peace that makes the soul resigned.
Only Time can bring the balm that calms the troubled mind.

All that I can do is pray that you'll be given power,
and the strength that you will need in this your bitter hour . . .
Words, I know, can't take away the pain another bears,
but I'm wanting you to know you're in my thoughts and prayers.

Pictures in the Fireside

What do you see in the fire tonight?
I see the oddest things:
A castle on a mountain-top
A bird with flaming wings.
An old man, a gnome I think,
A dwarf with pointed beard,
A cottage with three chimney pots.
A forest, wild and weird.
I see a ruby-studded cave,
With crimson stalactites.
And just behind that bit of coal
There are the strangest sights.
A lady with a basket
And a small boy with a dog.
Can't you see them seated there
Upon the apple log?

When I Remember You

I remember a thousand things when I remember you:
the firelight glowing on polished oak; a table set for two . . .
The gleam of lamps in a rain-washed street; the shimmer of wet
leaves.
The smoky grey of November nights. The blue of April eves.

A meeting under a station clock. A song, a smile, a dance.
The muted sweetness of violins; the music of romance . . .
A country walk and a cottage tea; a window with a view.
I remember a thousand things when I remember you.

Sharing

If we share we multiply the good things we possess.
If we share them we increase our joy and happiness . . .
If we cast our bread upon the stream of life's affairs
it may feed some hungry soul, or answer someone's prayers . . .
Time will bear it back to us, returning it will bring
a blessing and a joy unknown to those who clutch and cling
to what the good God give to them, the silver and the gold.
Things are only lent to us; they are not ours to hold.

If you hoard you block the channels. Let the good things flow.
Take with grateful joy the riches that the fates bestow.
Keep them not for selfish ends until the chance has gone.
Help to make God's gifts go round . . . and pass the blessings on.

Fireside Rendezvous

Dream-faces from the shadows smile at me,
when from the busy world I draw apart . . .
Ghosts cross the threshold of my memory
as I unlatch the doorways of the heart.

Draw the bright curtains on the twilight gloom.
Shut out the darkness as the night descends . . .
Here in the silence of this firelit room
I have a rendezvous with absent friends.

Think

Think before you cut the link that snaps the golden chain –
Pause before you take a step that causes others pain . . .
Wait before you speak the word that tears old bonds apart –
Listen to the voice of conscience in your secret heart.

Think before you cast aside affection tried and true,
and break the faith of someone who has loved and trusted you.

Try a Little Humour

Try a little humour when life's going wrong.
Try a little laughter, try a little song . . .
It will work like magic when you're feeling low –
make a little effort, and the mood will go.

Try a little sunshine on a gloomy day.
Practise painting rainbows on a sky of grey . . .
Don't sit at the window grumbling at the showers –
weave a thread of brightness through the dreary hours.

Do not be despondent when the shadows fall.
Brooding on your problems will not help at all . . .
Fight down the depression and your feelings hide.
Try a little humour, see the funny side.

Open the Window

Open the window and let in the sun.
The season of life and of light has begun.
Open the window. The wind is a broom
that sweeps out the cobwebs, the dust and the gloom.

Open the windows of hope. Fling them wide,
when it is cheerless and stuffy inside . . .
Germs of self-pity, of fear and of doubt
thrive in the darkness, so drive them all out.

Viewed from the shadows through windows shut fast,
the future is veiled in the fogs of the past . . .
But eyes that can see with a faith big and bold
look through the mists to horizons of gold.

A Wish For a Friend

Blessings be yours – and all felicity.
Come shine or shadow, happy may you be . . .
Every good gift may Fortune give to you:
hope, health and peace – and friendships fond and true.

Time grant to you the harvesting of dreams –
and may your path be lit with golden gleams,
so that you walk down bright and pleasant ways.
Light be your heart and sunny be your days.

Time

Tender and light is the touch of time upon the wound of grief . . .
Gentle the pressure of the years that bring the heart relief.

Time from our memories draws the sting – thus we forget the pain.
Only the sweetest recollections of the past remain.

Dark turns to dawn and sight to songs, harsh notes to harmony . . .
Death leads to life and love lives on through all eternity.

Someday Soon

Someday soon, if fate be kind, these lonely days will seem
like a long forgotten story – hazy as a dream.
Someday soon the sun will shine, the shadows all depart,
and the old sweet happiness steal back into the heart.

Someday soon we'll be together, side by side again.
Quickly then we will forget the past with all its pain,
as we face the future years afire with faith and zest,
hoping they will be for us the brightest and the best.

Sweet Is the Dream

Sweet is the dream that comes upon the tides of memory,
like a lovely ship afloat upon a quiet sea.
The dream in which I live again the unforgotten past –
the dream that never fails to come, and seems too sweet to last.

Waking, sleeping, it is there: the dream that has no end:
the thought of you, my dear companion and my heart's true friend.
From the evil of the world, its sorrow and distress –
I escape into my dreams, there find happiness.

Thoughts Go Home

Thoughts go home, unbidden – when we're somewhere far away.
Thoughts need no compelling. Off they wander, night or day,
to seek the places and the faces dear unto the heart:
the spot where all our journeys lead, and all roads end and start.

Thoughts go back. They know the way. They need no road or guide
to cross the hills and rivers and the oceans that divide . . .
And though with friends we may abide as round the world we roam,
to the place of heart's desire thoughts turn. Love leads them home.

Music

Music is a language, universal in its scope,
expressing every shade and tone of human fear and hope.
Bliss and grief and all that lies between those two extremes:
sorrow, wonder, exultation and unspoken dreams.

All mankind can know and grasp and understand these things:
the fingers on the keyboard, and the bow upon the strings . . .
Men need no interpreters their message to impart –
when they speak through music in the language of the heart.

When You Hope

When you hope, you turn your face
    away from sorrow and despair –
and you see the light of heaven
    that is shining everywhere.

When you hope, you lift a latch;
    a door swings back and you behold –
broader views and brighter prospects,
    fair green vistas touched with gold.

Though your heart is sad and troubled,
    doubt not in the bitter hour . . .
When you hope you prove your faith,
    acknowledging God's gracious power.

Between the Lines

When we write a letter to a dear one far away,
words fail to express the meanings that we would convey . . .
As the pen moves on the paper recollections start –
a face is pictured in the mind; a voice speaks in the heart.
Though we write of humdrum things and everyday affairs,
behind the words lie all our dreams, our longings and our prayers.
Hopes outpace the written word and thoughts leap on ahead.
And memory between the lines entwines her golden thread.

The Turning Point

There is a milestone on life's path
    that brings us to another start,
where brighter vistas open out,
    where clouds grow light and break apart . . .

There is a spot on every road
    where ruts give place to smooth green ways;
the place that marks a new beginning,
    and the hope of fairer days.

Are you weary of the journey –
    does your burden seem too great?
Are you fighting uphill battles,
    struggling with a hostile Fate?
The milestone at the turning point
    may be a few steps round the bend.
Courage! . . .This may be the spot
    where joys return and troubles end.

The Tapestry of Time

Life works out a pattern on the tapestry of Time.
The threads of hope, of love and grief, of fear and faith sublime,
of happiness and bitterness, of joy and misery,
are stitched into the great design of human destiny.

Within so vast a frame, our tiny patch we cannot see.
Too close we stand to trace the pattern on the tapestry.
But someday, looking from afar, perhaps we shall behold
our little bit of the design; our own small thread of gold.